The Heinemann Illustrated Encyclopedia

Volume 8

Pte-Slo

Heinemann
LIBRARY

First published in Great Britain by Heinemann Library
Halley Court, Jordan Hill, Oxford OX2 8EJ
a division of Reed Educational and Professional Publishing Ltd.

OXFORD MELBOURNE AUCKLAND
JOHANNESBURG BLANTYRE GABORONE
IBADAN PORTSMOUTH NH (USA) CHICAGO

Series Editors: Rebecca and Stephen Vickers
Author Team: Rob Alcraft, Catherine Chambers, Jim Drake,
Fred Martin, Angela Royston, Jane Shuter, Roger Thomas,
Rebecca Vickers, Stephen Vickers
Reading Consultant: Betty Root

Photo research by Katharine Smith
Designed and Typeset by Gecko Ltd
Printed in Hong Kong by Wing King Tong

02 01 00 99 98
10 9 8 7 6 5 4 3 2 1

ISBN 0 431 09059 9

British Library Cataloguing in Publication Data.

The Heinemann illustrated encyclopedia
   1. Children's encyclopedias and dictionaries
   I. Vickers, Rebecca II. Vickers, Stephen, 1951–
032

ISBN 0431090629

Acknowledgements:
Cover: The cover illustration is of a male specimen of *Ornithoptera goliath*, commonly called the Goliath Birdwing.
Special thanks to Dr George C. McGavin and the Hope Entomological Collections, Oxford University Museum of
Natural History.

J. Allan Cash Ltd: pp13L, 21b, 25, 27, 29, 41b, 42, 44, 47, 48. **British Museum:** p30r. **Bruce Coleman Ltd.:** Dr
Eckart Pott – p38t. **EPS Press:** p11b. **Forest Life Picture Library:** p30L. **The Hutchison Library:** pp18t, 26, 43b;
L. Taylor – p43t. **Kobal Collection:** p20t. **Mansell Collection:** p11t. **Natural History Museum:** Mary Anning –
p4. **Oxford Scientific Film:** Harold Taylor Abipp – p38b; Doug Allan – p37t; G.I. Bernard – p8b; Martyn Colbeck –
p34t. J.A.L. Cook – p28b; Mary Deebie and Victoria Stone – p34b; Warren Faidley – p12b; Carol Farnetti – p14b;
David Fritts – p17b; Peter Gathercole – 18b; Howard Hall – p15b; Richard | Hermann – p35b; Rudie Kuiter – p32;
Zig Leszczynski – p9b; C.K. Lorenz – p9t; T.C. Middleston – p21t; Sean Morris – p13r; William Paton – p8t; Press-Tige
Pictures – p14b; Richard Ray – p46t; L.L.T. Rhodes – p40b; James Robinson – p36r; Norbert Rosing – p37b; Kjell
Sandved – p35t; Wendy Shattil and Bob Rozinski – p46b; David Tipling – p36L; Steve Turner – p17t; Tom Ulrich –
p41t; P. and W. Ward – p28t; Barrie Watts – p31t; Doug Wechsler – p31b; Babs and Bert Wells – 16b; Robert Wu – p33t.
Picturepoint: p6b. **Science Photo Library:** . p45b; John Mead – p10t. **Still Pictures:** John Concalori – 16t.
Tony Stone Worldwide: Simeone Huber – p7; Gavriel Jecan – p22. **Werner Forman Archive:** p6t. **Zefa:** p19b.

Every effort has been made to contact copyright holders of any material
reproduced in this book. Any omissions will be rectified in subsequent printings
if notice is given to the Publisher.

Welcome to the
Heinemann Illustrated Encyclopedia

What is an encyclopedia?

An encyclopedia is an information book. It gives the most important facts about a lot of different subjects. This encyclopedia has been specially written for children your age. It covers many of the subjects from school and others you may find interesting.

What is in this encyclopedia?

In this encyclopedia each topic is called an entry. There is one page for every entry. The entries in this encyclopedia are on:

- animals
- plants
- dinosaurs
- countries
- geography
- history
- world religions
- music
- art
- transport
- science
- technology

How to use this encyclopedia

This encyclopedia has eleven books, called volumes. The first ten volumes contain entries. The entries are all in alphabetical order. This means that Volume One starts with entries that begin with the letter 'A' and Volume Ten ends with entries that begin with the letter 'Z'. Volume Eleven is the index volume and has some other interesting information in its Fact Finder section.

Here are two entries, showing you what you can find on a page:

The See also *line tells you where to find other related information.*

This is the letter that the entry starts with.

Fact boxes give you details about the topic.

Did You Know? boxes have fun or interesting bits of information.

The Fact File tells you important facts and figures.

Pterosaur

See also: Dinosaur, Fossil

The pterosaurs were flying lizards which lived at the time of the dinosaurs. They had leathery wings, without feathers. Their long, bony tails helped them steer. There were many different kinds of pterosaur.

Lifestyle

Some pterosaurs, like the pterodactyl, were small and fast flying. Others, like the pteranodon, were giants. Their wings were seven metres across, as big as a small aircraft. The giant pteranodon could swoop down and scoop up fish from rivers or lakes. It is thought that pterodactyls also caught flying insects.

FACTS

COLOUR....not known
SIZE.......... from 20 cm to 11 m
WEIGHT....up to 25 kg
BIGGEST.... Quetzalcoatlus
(11m long)

Long fourth finger to hold the leathery wing

A Rhamphorhynchus pterosaur

Long, bony tail to help the pterosaur to steer

fourth finger

This fossil of a Dimorphodon pterosaur shows the long fourth finger bone that held up the leathery wing.

FOOD

Pterosaurs had rows of spiky teeth that helped them to catch fish and insects.

Puerto Rico

See also: North America,
United States of America

Puerto Rico is a country in the Caribbean Sea. It is a group of islands. The largest island has mountains. There is flat land near the coast in the north and south. The climate is warm, windy and wet.

Living and working

Most people in Puerto Rico live in the cities and towns, working in factories and offices, or helping the tourists. On the farms coffee, vegetables, sugar cane, rice and bananas are grown.

The people of Puerto Rico are a mixture of African, Spanish and local Native Americans. Most of the population are Roman Catholic Christians and there are many colourful religious festivals and saints' days. One of the most important is the 'Festival of Innocents' where there are costumes and floats.

This man is wearing a special costume for the Festival of the Innocents. He has won a prize.

DID YOU KNOW?

Puerto Rico has a special relationship with the United States. It is sometimes called the '51st state'.

FACT FILE

NORTH AMERICA

PEOPLE	Puerto Ricans
POPULATION	3.6 million
MAIN LANGUAGES	Spanish, English
CAPITAL CITY	San Juan
MONEY	US dollar
HIGHEST MOUNTAIN	Cerro de Punta – 1338 m
LONGEST RIVER	Grand de Arecibo – 65 km

Puppetry

See also: Drama, Theatre

Puppetry is a way of telling stories using dolls called puppets. The person who moves them is called a puppeteer.

Types of puppet

Puppets can be moved in different ways. Glove puppets fit on the puppeteer's hand like a glove. Puppets can also be moved with strings, on sticks, or electronically. Some puppets are cut from flat shapes and have a light shining behind them so that the puppets show up as shadows.

How puppets are used

Puppets are often used to tell stories to children. In some countries, such as Japan, puppet shows are also put on especially for adults.

Puppets are still a popular way of telling a story. New puppet shows are being invented all the time, for live performances and for television. Famous puppeteers include Jim Henson, who during his life created the Muppets, and Gerry Anderson, who invented the puppets in many space adventure stories.

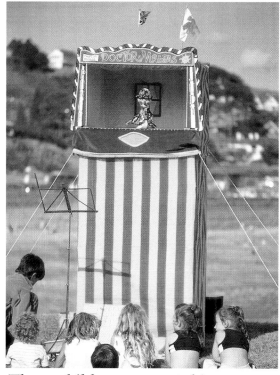

These children are watching a Punch and Judy show. It is about Punch and his wife, Judy. In these stories, Punch fights with Judy, a policeman and a crocodile – he fights with everybody.

These puppets, from Java in Indonesia, are used to tell folktales. They are moved by sticks.

DID YOU KNOW?

Puppets which hang from strings are called marionettes.

Pyramid

See also: Egypt, Egypt (Ancient), Maya

Pyramids are buildings that were first made by the Ancient Egyptians, about 3500 years ago. The first pyramids had square bases and sides that went up to a point, in steps. Later, pyramids had smooth sides.

What were pyramids for?

The pyramids were huge tombs built for the Ancient Egyptian rulers, who were called the pharaohs. The Ancient Egyptians believed people had another life after they died, so they needed their bodies to be buried with food and everyday things.

The Egyptian pyramids were so well built that they are still standing.

KEY DATES

2660 BC....	The first step pyramid was built in Ancient Egypt
2600 BC....	The first smooth-sided pyramid was built in Ancient Egypt
2580 BC....	The Great Pyramid was built at Giza
1500 BC....	The Ancient Egyptians began to bury their pharaohs in tombs, not pyramids
AD 500......	The Maya built step pyramid temples

Mummies

Because they believed people still needed their bodies, the Ancient Egyptians tried to make sure that dead bodies did not rot away. To do this, they took out the soft insides of the dead person, then they dried out the body. They wrapped it in bandages soaked in oil.

A body that has been treated like this is called a mummy. When it was dried, the mummy was put in a specially-shaped wooden box, which was painted with a face to look like the person inside. This special box is called a *sarcophagus*.

DID YOU KNOW?

The Maya people of central America built pyramids as temples to their gods. Their pyramids always had steps, so people could climb to the temple on the flat top.

Rabbit

See also: Mammal

A rabbit is a small long-eared mammal which is often kept as a pet. It can run very fast. Some kinds can run up to 40 kph, and can hop a long way in one leap. A rabbit usually sleeps in the day and comes out at night. There are rabbits living all around the world.

Rabbit families

Some kinds of rabbit live together with many others in a large network of underground tunnels called a warren. Other rabbits live on their own. A male rabbit is called a buck. A female rabbit is called a doe. A baby rabbit is sometimes called a kitten or a bunny.

Female rabbits have several litters of five to eight babies each year. Some rabbits have their babies underground, but others make nests in the grass.

These bunnies are six days old. They haven't opened their eyes yet.

RABBIT FACTS

NUMBER OF	
KINDS	44 rabbits and hares
COLOUR	brownish-grey – pet rabbits can be many colours
LENGTH	up to 60 cm
WEIGHT	up to 5 kg
STATUS	common
LIFE SPAN	up to 6 years
ENEMIES	foxes, snakes, eagles, people

Sensitive nose to smell friends and enemies

Long ears to listen for danger

A European rabbit

Strong back legs for hopping and running

FOOD

A rabbit eats mostly grass, clover and herbs. In winter the rabbit eats bark, twigs and seeds. Rabbits that live near the seaside eat seaweed.

Racoon

See also: Mammal

A racoon is a furry mammal. It has black stripes round its tail and a black face mask. Racoons live near trees and water in North and South America. They can swim and climb well.

Racoon families

The female racoon has up to three babies. They are called kits. The mother feeds the kits on milk. When they are older, she teaches them to fish with their front paws.

In summer racoons usually live on their own or in small groups made up of a mother and her kits. In winter racoons crowd together in dens to keep warm.

RACOON FACTS

NUMBER OF KINDS...	1
COLOUR	grey and black
WEIGHT	up to 15 kg
LENGTH	up to 1 m
STATUS	common
LIFE SPAN	up to 10 years
ENEMIES	people

Sharp teeth for tearing food and crushing crab shells

A racoon

Tail for balance while climbing

Hands for feeling and gripping

These kits are staying near their den.

FOOD

Racoons usually come out at night. They hunt for eggs up in the trees, and they hunt for crabs, frogs and fish in water. Racoons are wild animals, but they often live near people. They like to move into areas where people have their houses, and search through dustbins for food.

Radio

See also: Communication, Television

Radio is an important method of communication. It uses radio waves that are sent from a transmitter to a receiver. Receivers are usually radio sets like the ones in cars and homes.

The first radio system

The first radio system was made by Guglielmo Marconi in 1895. In 1901 he worked out how to send a radio signal across the Atlantic Ocean, from England to the USA. After a few years, most big ships had radios. A ship could now send messages if it was in trouble, far out at sea. By the 1920s public radio was popular. It broadcast news, music and other entertainment.

All radio transmitters, like this one in Australia, are very tall so that the signals don't get blocked by hills or buildings.

How radio systems work

Each radio signal is different. All signals have their own frequency. The frequency is the number of radio waves that arrive every second. When someone tunes a radio they choose one frequency. They can only hear the station transmitting on that frequency.

DID YOU KNOW?

Televisions and mobile telephones use radio signals. Communication satellites receive radio signals from one place on Earth and bounce them back to another place on Earth.

This radio receiver can pick up programmes on three different wavelengths. It is powered by batteries. Small battery radios were first available in 1955.

Railway

See also: Train, Transport

A railway is a track made for trains to run along. Railways join cities, factories and ports. They carry people and goods. The first railways were built 200 years ago.

RAILWAY FACTS

FIRST PUBLIC RAILWAY	opened in 1801 in London, England
LONGEST ROUTE	9,438 km from Moscow to Nakhodka in Russia
BIGGEST STATION	Grand Central Station in New York, USA, with 67 tracks on two levels

The first railways

The first railways had wooden tracks. There were no trains, just horses pulling boxes of coal. Then the steam engine was invented. It was powerful and could work much faster than horses or people. Railways became longer, joining more places and carrying more people. Today there are railways through mountain tunnels and even under the sea.

After the last spike was driven into the track on May 10th 1869, a railway line crossed the United States from the Atlantic to the Pacific.

People and railways

As railways spread, people found they could travel a long way, very quickly. Goods could get to places far from where they were made. Fresh food could travel long distances without going bad. Cities and towns grew, just because the railway had arrived.

This modern European electric-powered train runs on tracks designed for trains travelling at high speed.

Rainbow

See also: Colour, Light

A rainbow is made by lights of different colours when white sunlight shines through raindrops. When it shines through the drops of water, the light is split up into different colours. This is called the colour spectrum of light.

How is a rainbow made?

The colours in a rainbow are all in the sunlight that we see. Light from the sun is seen as white light, but it is really made up of a mixture of red, orange, yellow, green, blue, indigo and violet light.

When sunlight hits a raindrop it bends. Each coloured light is bent by a different amount. This separates the colours to form a spectrum.

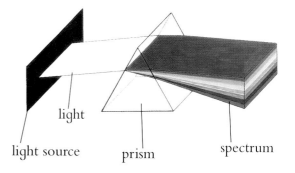

light

light source   prism   spectrum

A rain drop acts like this prism. When the light hits it, it divides the colours of light into a spectrum.

How to see a rainbow

A rainbow only appears if the sun is at least halfway down the sky, towards the horizon. When the sun shines during a shower of rain, turn, so that the sun is behind you and look straight ahead. The rainbow arch will be bigger if the sun is lower.

DID YOU KNOW?

You can never find the place where a rainbow comes to the ground. This is because a rainbow is a trick of the light, and can only be seen from a distance.

This rainbow will fade away as the rain stops falling, or if the sun goes behind clouds.

Rainforest

See also: Forest, Plant

Rainforests are very important for the Earth. Many different plants and animals live in rainforests. A lot of them are useful to people. Most rainforests are in the hot and wet tropical areas.

Tropical rainforests

Tropical rainforests have five layers. At the bottom there are small plants, such as mosses and ferns, and rich soil made of all the rotted leaves. Small animals and insects live here. The next layer is shrubs and larger ferns. The next layer is the middle layer, where there are young trees.

The canopy, which is about 30 metres high, is thick and green and is made up of the tops of the fully grown trees. A few very tall trees poke up through the canopy to form the fifth layer, called the emergent layer.

This tropical rainforest along the Amazon River in Brazil has different plants and animals living in each layer.

Temperate rainforests

In some parts of the USA, Europe, Australia and the cool, wet parts of Africa, there are temperate rainforests. The trees are mainly the type that lose their leaves in winter.

This cool, damp, temperate rainforest is in Washington state in the United States.

DID YOU KNOW?

A lot of the rainforests of the world are being cut down. An area nearly as big as England is cut down every year. If this continues, there will soon be no rainforests.

Rat

See also: Mammal

A rat is a quick, four-legged mammal. Rats are clever, and can learn to live anywhere. They have followed humans round the world. They live in cities and houses where it is warm and there is plenty of food. Rats also live in the countryside. Rats can spread diseases such as plague and typhoid. These diseases can kill people.

Rat families

Rats have lots of babies. One pair of rats can produce many babies in a lifetime. The female can have a litter of about fourteen babies, three times every year. She feeds the babies with milk, until they are old enough to look for food. In the countryside, rats live in groups called colonies.

RAT FACTS

NUMBER OF KINDS	1082 mice and rats
COLOUR	usually brown or grey
LENGTH	up to 50 cm
STATUS	common
LIFE SPAN	up to 5 years
ENEMIES	dogs, cats, people

A brown rat

Large flaps protect the sensitive ears

Strong, hairless, muscular tail for balance

Claws and strong legs for running and climbing

Whiskers to feel the sides of small spaces in the dark, so it doesn't get trapped

FOOD

Rats have front teeth that never stop growing. As they wear down, the teeth sharpen themselves. Rats eat grain, fruit, rubbish and scraps. They often steal food from humans, or they get into food that is being stored.

This Acacia rat from Botswana in Africa lives with her family in a tree.

Ray

See also: Fish, Sea life

A ray is a special kind of fish. Instead of fins, it has a flat body with wide wings. It swims through the water by flapping these wings. Rays live in oceans all over the world. Some rays have poisonous stings on their tails for protection.

Ray families

Big rays, such as manta rays, swim around the sea on their own. Smaller kinds, like stingrays, gather close together in groups. Rays do not have homes, but some rays spend a lot of time hiding in the sand on the bottom of the sea. Female rays do not lay eggs. They give birth to about ten live babies. The babies can look after themselves as soon as they are born.

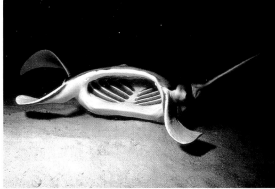

This manta ray has its mouth open, showing the filter plates used to catch small animals in the water.

RAY FACTS

NUMBER OF KINDS	425
COLOUR	different colours on top, white underneath
LENGTH	up to 5 m
WEIGHT	manta ray – up to 1360 kg
STATUS	common
LIFE SPAN	up to 20 years
ENEMIES	people

Wings for swimming

Flexible (bendy) tail with poisonous sting for protection

A stingray

Eyes on the top of the head for seeing things when hiding in sand

Flat body for hiding in sand

FOOD

Manta rays eat shrimp, plankton or small fish, which they filter from the water. Stingrays eat sea worms, shellfish and crabs.

Reptile

See also: Animals

A reptile is a cold-blooded animal, with scaly skin. Snakes, crocodiles, lizards and tortoises are all kinds of reptile. Reptiles can live on the land and in water. They live all around the world, except in the coldest places.

Types of reptile

There are four main groups of reptile: **Alligators and crocodiles** – These are the biggest reptiles.

Lizards and snakes – There are more than 5000 kinds of lizards and snakes around the world. This is the biggest group of reptiles.

Tortoises and turtles – These are protected by their hard shells. The shell of the Galapagos giant tortoise can be 1.5 metres long.

Tuatara – These are very rare. Tuataras live only on the North Island of New Zealand.

FOOD

All reptiles are hunters and eat meat, fish and insects. Reptiles don't heat their own blood. They don't need much energy, so they don't have to eat much. Many reptiles can go without food for months, or even years.

REPTILE FACTS

NUMBER OF KINDS	over 6000
LONGEST LIVED	Marion's tortoise, 152 years
LARGEST	Leatherback turtle, 752 kg

A tuatara from New Zealand.

This Wheeler's Gecko is a type of lizard. It has sticky pads on its feet so it can crawl up and down vertical surfaces.

Rhinoceros

See also: Mammal

A rhinoceros is a large, horned mammal. A rhinoceros is also called a rhino. It has thick skin like armour. Three kinds of rhino live in Asia, and have one horn each. They are all very rare. Two kinds live in Africa, and have two horns each.

RHINOCEROS FACTS

NUMBER OF KINDS	5
COLOUR	grey
HEIGHT	up to 2 m
LENGTH	up to 3.8 m
WEIGHT	up to 2200 kg
STATUS	endangered
LIFE SPAN	20–50 years
ENEMIES	lions, hyenas, tigers, people

Rhinoceros families

A rhinoceros lives on its own in grassland, but shares a water-hole or mud wallow with other rhinos. A male rhino is called a bull and a female is called a cow. A cow only has one calf at a time. Bull rhinos fight over land, but they let females and calves come in to their territory. A cow looks after her calf for two to five years.

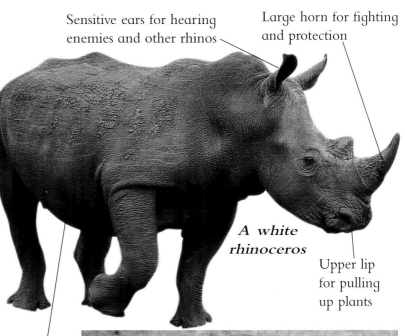

Sensitive ears for hearing enemies and other rhinos

Large horn for fighting and protection

A white rhinoceros

Upper lip for pulling up plants

Thick skin for protection

FOOD

A rhinoceros eats branches, leaves, fruit, grass and herbs.

This female black rhinoceros feeding her calf has a very long horn.

River

See also: Delta, Flood, Valley

A river is a flow of water that drains off the land. Rivers carry water from the land to the sea. A small river is called a stream.

Why rivers flow

The water in rivers comes from rain and melting snow. Some rivers start from a lake or marsh in the mountains. Others start at a spring where water flows out of the rocks from under the ground.

Streams and rivers flow into each other to make bigger rivers. A stream or river that flows into a bigger river is called a tributary. Rivers wash away soil and rocks, and make valleys.

People and rivers

People use rivers for drinking water and for watering crops. They also use rivers for bathing, washing clothes, fishing and travelling. Fast-flowing rivers and waterfalls can also be used to generate electricity.

DID YOU KNOW?

The river with the most water flowing down it is the River Amazon in South America. The Amazon is nearly 6450 kilometres long.

Some rivers make large bends called meanders.

People fish in rivers for food and for fun.

Road

See also: Transport

A road is a pathway used by people to get from one place to another. Today there are many new, fast roads. There are also some roads that follow paths made thousands of years ago.

The first roads

Roads were simple paths used by many people and animals. They were usually the shortest or easiest way to get from one place to another. These roads were just hard earth, pushed down by people walking along them. When it rained they turned into mud.

The Ancient Romans built the first proper road system. These roads were hard, level and were easy to use in all weathers. They were made for soldiers to walk on. Today's roads are made for wheeled vehicles such as buses, cars and lorries.

People and roads

Most people use roads every day. Roads make travel easy, but the traffic on them can cause air pollution. They are also expensive to design, build and repair.

DID YOU KNOW?

The Ancient Roman roads were always built as straight as possible.

ROAD FIRSTS

FIRST RECOGNIZED ROAD	Persia, 3500 BC
FIRST MOTORWAY	Italy, 1924
FIRST PAVED ROAD	England, 1835

This is a turnpike road in England about 175 years ago. People had to pay to use turnpikes. The money was used to repair them.

Some modern road systems have complicated junctions. The roads that go on top are called flyovers. The ones that go underneath are called underpasses.

Robot

See also: Computer, Laser, Space exploration

A robot is a machine that can be given instructions (programmed) to do certain jobs. They are often controlled by computers. Most robots are used in factories. They can do boring, heavy or dangerous jobs without getting tired.

How robots work

A robot has to be told what to do. The instructions are usually in a computer program. The robot stores the program. It will then do the same job again and again. If the robot is to do a different job, its program must be changed.

One day it may be possible to make robots as clever as C3PO and R2D2, from the film Star Wars.

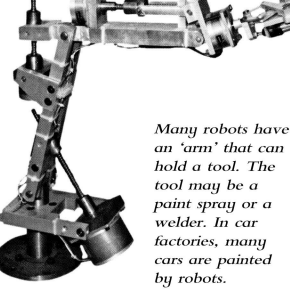

Many robots have an 'arm' that can hold a tool. The tool may be a paint spray or a welder. In car factories, many cars are painted by robots.

Robots and space exploration

Robots can go on journeys through space that take years, and can survive where people would die. Robot space probes have gone to every planet in the solar system, except Pluto.

DID YOU KNOW?

Scientists are trying to make robots that can be programmed to think. When a computer or robot thinks, this is called 'artificial intelligence'.

Rocks

See also: Metal, Mining

Rocks are all the solid, non-living things that make up the Earth. Rocks take many millions of years to form. They are on and under the ground everywhere in the world. There are many different types of rock. Some are very hard. Others are quite soft.

The three kinds of rock

Igneous rock: Deep inside the Earth there is no solid rock, only a hot liquid called magma. If magma comes near to the surface, or erupts through a volcano, it cools down and sets solid. This makes igneous rocks. They are usually hard and don't wear away quickly.

Sedimentary rock: These soft rocks were mostly formed in lakes or oceans. Some were made from layers of sand or mud. Others were made from the tiny shells of lake or sea creatures. Over millions of years they get squashed down into rock.

Metamorphic rocks: When sedimentary rock gets heated and squashed, near a volcano, it changes into metamorphic rock. These rocks are usually harder than sedimentary rocks.

This chalk is a sedimentary rock. It has been eroded by the sea.

DID YOU KNOW?

Rocks are made of minerals. Some minerals are metals, such as iron, gold, copper and silver. Other minerals, such as salt, sulphur and quartz are non-metals (not metals).

Slate is a metamorphic rock made from layers of heated mud. Slate can be split into tiles for roofs.

Romania

See also: Europe

Romania is a country in the south-east of Europe. It has a coast along the Black Sea. Mountains go through the middle of Romania. The River Danube flows through the south. The weather is cold and dry in winter with warm summers. There are big forests with deer and wild boar.

The stories about Count Dracula come from this part of southern Romania, called Transylvania.

Living and working

About one-third of the people in Romania work on farms. Farmers grow wheat, maize, sugar beet and vegetables. They also raise herds of cattle and sheep.

People make goods from chemicals, cement and metals. Pollution from factories is a problem.

DID YOU KNOW?

At least 300 kinds of birds live in the Danube delta. Many birds stop there as they fly south for the winter.

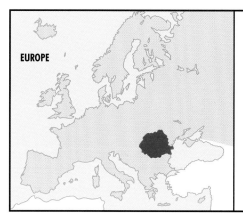

EUROPE

FACT FILE

PEOPLE.........................Romanians
POPULATION...............22.9 million
MAIN LANGUAGE.........Romanian
CAPITAL CITY.............Bucharest
MONEY.......................Leu
HIGHEST MOUNTAIN...Mount Moldoveanu – 2544m
LONGEST RIVER..........River Danube – 2850 km

Rome, Ancient

See also: Italy, Road

The Roman Empire began as the city of Rome, in Italy. The Romans built up a huge empire by taking over other lands. The Roman Empire was at its largest in AD 120.

What was Ancient Rome like?

At first, Rome was ruled by kings. As the empire grew it was run by a group of people. Finally, it was ruled by an emperor, who had all the power. The Ancient Romans are famous for their Latin language and their roads.

KEY DATES

753 BC................	The city of Rome set up
250 BC................	Romans control Italy
250 BC–AD 120...	Romans take over more land in Europe, Asia and North Africa
AD 284................	The Roman Empire splits into two parts

What happened to Ancient Rome?

The Roman Empire grew too big to be ruled properly from Rome. It split into two parts in AD 284. From then on, the Roman Empire shrank as other countries and empires formed.

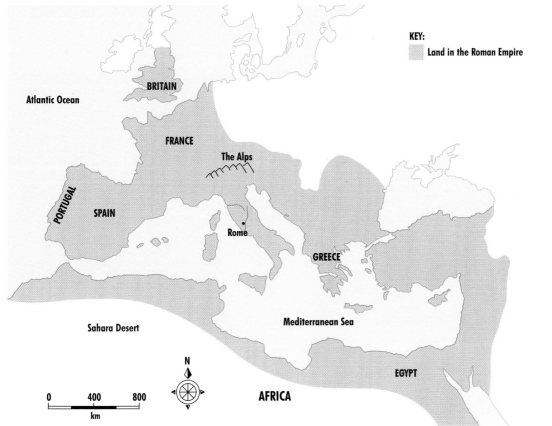

The Roman Empire at its peak.

Root

See also: Plant

The roots of a plant are the parts that normally grow under the ground. Roots take in water and hold the plant in the soil.

The life of a root

The root is usually the first part of a plant to grow from a seed. The tip of the root pushes down through the soil. Some plants have a large main root called a taproot. Other plants produce a network of roots which grow in all directions.

Many vegetables, such as carrots, sweet potatoes, beetroot, cassava and yams are roots. These swollen roots are stores of food for the plant.

All plant roots help to hold soil in place. They stop it being blown away by the wind or washed away by the rain.

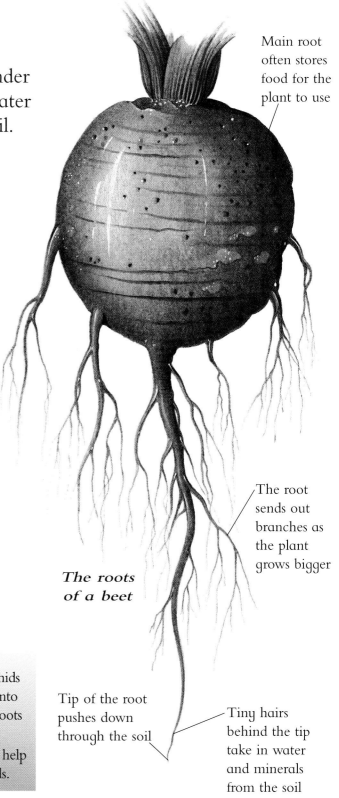

Main root often stores food for the plant to use

The root sends out branches as the plant grows bigger

The roots of a beet

Tip of the root pushes down through the soil

Tiny hairs behind the tip take in water and minerals from the soil

DID YOU KNOW?

Some roots never go underground. Orchids have aerial roots that help them hold onto the bigger plants they grow on. Aerial roots take in water out of the air.

Ivy has many small climbing roots that help it cling on as it climbs up trees and walls.

Russia

See also: Asia, Europe

Russia is a very large country, with parts in Europe and Asia. The Ural Mountains divide Europe from Asia. The north of Russia is inside the Arctic Circle. It is dry and much warmer in the south.

Living and working

The best farmland in Russia is in the west where farmers grow wheat, potatoes and other crops. They also keep cattle. There is mining for coal, oil, gas and metals. Factory workers make everything, from matchsticks to microwaves. Most people in the cities live in blocks of flats. About one-quarter of the people in Russia live in the countryside. In the forests, some people still live in traditional wooden huts called *izba*.

Many different groups of people live in Russia. Each group has its own customs, music and dancing.

St. Basil's Cathedral in Moscow's Red Square is famous for its 'onion' roofs. There is a big parade in Red Square in Moscow on 1 May every year.

DID YOU KNOW?

Until 1991, Russia and fourteen smaller countries together formed the Soviet Union.

EUROPE

ASIA

FACT FILE

PEOPLE	Russians
POPULATION	147.4 million
MAIN LANGUAGE	Russian
CAPITAL CITY	Moscow
MONEY	Rouble
HIGHEST MOUNTAIN	Elbrus – 5642 m
LONGEST RIVER	Yenisey–Angara – 5550 km

Rwanda

See also: Africa

Rwanda is a small country in the middle of Africa. There are mountains and forests, and it is warm and wet all year round.

Living and working

Most families in Rwanda live in small houses they build themselves. These houses have mud walls, and roofs made from the leaves of banana trees. Most will also have a small garden, where the family grow their own food. They grow bananas, sweet potatoes and a plant called cassava. The roots of the cassava plant are used to make flour. Some farmers grow coffee and tea which is then sold to other countries.

There are two main tribes, or groups, in Rwanda. They are called the Hutu and the Tutsi. Fights started in 1994 between the Hutu and the Tutsi. Many people in Rwanda have been killed in fighting between the Hutus and the Tutsi. The fighting has made life in Rwanda hard.

These Tutsi dancers are very tall. The Twa people, known as Pygmies, also live in Rwanda. They are some of the smallest people in the world. So, Rwanda has some of the tallest, as well as the shortest, people on Earth.

DID YOU KNOW?

Mountain gorillas in Rwanda are an endangered species. Fighting in the country and poachers killing gorillas mean very few are left.

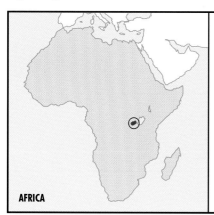

AFRICA

FACT FILE

PEOPLE	Rwandans
POPULATION	5.5 million
CAPITAL CITY	Kigali
MAIN LANGUAGES	Kinyarwanda and French
MONEY	Rwandan franc
HIGHEST MOUNTAIN	Mount Karisimbi – 4507 m
LONGEST RIVER	Kagera – 400 km

R

Saudi Arabia

See also: Asia

Saudi Arabia is a country in the Middle East. There are mountains in the west. Most of Saudi Arabia is a hot desert, with sand dunes, stones and bare rock. Snakes, lizards, rats and wild cats live in the desert.

Living and working

About half the people work in farming. Farmers grow crops such as wheat, bananas and dates in the areas where there is water. Some have herds of goats and camels. There is oil in the rocks under Saudi Arabia. The oil is sold to other countries to earn money.

Almost everyone in Saudi Arabia is a follower of the religion of Islam. The holy city of Islam, Makkah, is in Saudi Arabia. Followers of Islam try to make a special journey, called a pilgrimage, to this city once in their life. Many people save up for years until they can afford it.

At this market in Saudi Arabia all goods of one type are sold together. Here leather goods are on sale.

DID YOU KNOW?

The Saudi flag has Arabic writing on it. It is one of only a few national flags that have words included on them.

ASIA

FACT FILE

PEOPLE...................... Saudis
POPULATION............... 17.5 million
CAPITAL CITY.............. Riyadh
MAIN LANGUAGE......... Arabic
MONEY...................... Saudi riyal
HIGHEST MOUNTAIN....Jabal Sawda – 3133 m

Scorpion

See also: Invertebrate

A scorpion is a small animal with two large claws on its front legs, and six other legs. It has a curved tail with a sharp sting on the end. It is from the same group of animals as the spider. Scorpions are hunters, and live mainly in warm parts of the world.

SCORPION FACTS

NUMBER OF KINDS	over 1400
COLOUR	black or brown
LENGTH	1–18 cm
WEIGHT	up to 5 g
STATUS	rare
ENEMIES	owls, frogs, snakes, rats

Scorpion families

Female scorpions have lots of babies. They look just like tiny, see-through adult scorpions.

In the daytime scorpions hide under rocks or in holes. It is cool and damp in dark places, away from the heat of the sun.

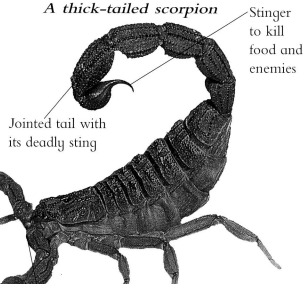

A thick-tailed scorpion

Stinger to kill food and enemies

Jointed tail with its deadly sting

Strong claws for grabbing food

Jaws for tearing food into small pieces

Babies ride around on the mother's back for about a year until they can look after themselves.

FOOD

Scorpions hunt at night. They use their poisonous stings to kill insects, centipedes, spiders and lizards. Scorpions can live in the driest places. They can go without water for months, and can live without food for more than a year.

Scotland

See also: United Kingdom

Scotland is one of the four main parts of the United Kingdom. Mountains cover much of Scotland. There are many long inlets and islands around the west coast.

Living and working

The two biggest cities in Scotland are Glasgow and Edinburgh. Not many people live in the mountains or on the islands. Some people make a living by farming and fishing. Others look after the tourists in hotels.

Scottish people sometimes wear clothes made from a special patterned woollen cloth called tartan. Each family, or clan, has a different pattern and colours.

Every year the Scottish highland games include some unusual sports. This sportsman wearing a tartan kilt is throwing the hammer.

DID YOU KNOW?

Loch Ness, a lake in the Scottish Highlands, is famous for the sightings of a large, unknown animal, sometimes called the Loch Ness Monster. Some people believe it is a real animal, but others don't think it exists at all.

EUROPE

FACT FILE

PEOPLE...................... Scots, Scottish

POPULATION.............. 5.1 million

MAIN LANGUAGES....... English and Scots Gaelic

CAPITAL CITY............ Edinburgh

MONEY...................... Pound sterling

HIGHEST MOUNTAIN... Ben Nevis – 1344 m

LONGEST RIVER.......... River Clyde – 160 km

Sculpture

See also: Art

Sculpture is works of art such as statues and other objects. A sculpture can show a real object. It can also be an image which conveys a feeling or an idea. A person who makes sculptures is called a sculptor.

Making sculptures

Sculpture can be made of almost any material. Very hard materials, such as stone or metal, are often used because they last a long time. Stone and wood are chipped and carved. Metal, plaster and plastic sculptures are usually made by pouring liquid into a mould.

DID YOU KNOW?

The earliest known sculptures are about 30,000 years old. One of the oldest is a carving of a horse from prehistoric times. It was found in a cave in Germany.

This huge wooden sculpture of a chair is on display in a forest. It is made from wood grown in the forest.

A sculpture of a human or animal figure is called a statue. Statues, like this one, were sometimes used in Ancient Greece and Ancient Rome as columns on buildings.

Sea anemone

See also: Sea life

A sea anemone is a sea animal with a soft body. It has no bones. Different sea anemones live in shallow seas and rockpools near the seashore all over the world. They are members of the same group of animals as jellyfish and corals.

Sea anemone families

Some sea anemones lay eggs to make baby anemones. Other kinds divide off parts of their own bodies to make more anemones. A sucker keeps the sea anemone stuck down. It will spend most of its life in the same place.

SEA ANEMONE FACTS

NUMBER OF KINDS..............	over 9000
COLOUR.........	all
LENGTH..........	3–7 cm
STATUS............	common
LIFE SPAN........	up to 100s of years
ENEMIES..........	sea slugs, fish

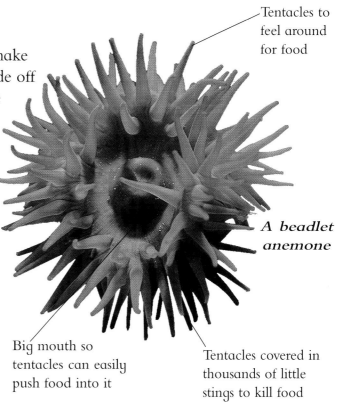

Tentacles to feel around for food

A beadlet anemone

Big mouth so tentacles can easily push food into it

Tentacles covered in thousands of little stings to kill food

This green sea anemone is eating a crab.

FOOD

Sea anemones are meat-eaters. They stick to rocks and use the stingers on the tentacles around their mouths to catch and kill animals such as shrimp and small fish. The tentacles push the food into the open mouth.

Sea horse

See also: Fish

A sea horse is a very strange fish. Its head looks like a horse's head. It has a curved tail and a long mouth like a drinking straw. Sea horses live in warm seas all over the world.

Sea horse families

Female sea horses lay eggs in the male sea horse. He has a special pouch to hold the eggs. When the eggs hatch the male sea horse opens the pouch to let the babies swim out.

FOOD

Sea horses are too slow to chase and catch food. So, to catch their food they stay perfectly still and wait. To help them stay hidden, sea horses change colour to match where they are. When small shrimp or little fish swim by the sea horse sucks them up like a vacuum cleaner.

SEA HORSE FACTS

NUMBER OF KINDS.............	35
COLOUR.........	changes to match surroundings
LENGTH..........	up to 30 cm
STATUS............	common
ENEMIES..........	other fish, people

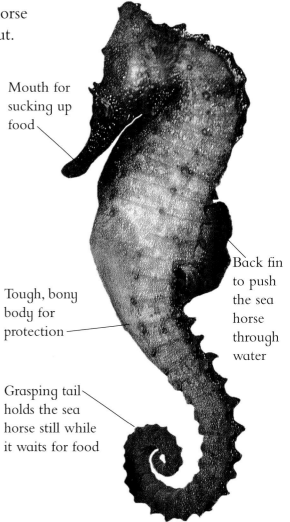

Mouth for sucking up food

Back fin to push the sea horse through water

Tough, bony body for protection

Grasping tail holds the sea horse still while it waits for food

A White's sea horse

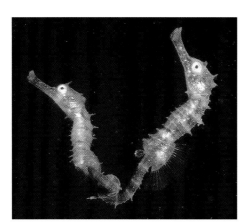

These newly hatched short-snouted sea horses are able to swim away as soon as they are born.

Sea life

See also: Coast, Coral, Fish

Most of the world is covered with sea. Many plants and animals live or feed in the sea. Most sea life is near the top of the water, where there is plenty of light. Some creatures live in the deep sea, where it is dark.

Living in the sea

Plants and animals need oxygen to live. Most sea animals can take oxygen from the water. Sea plants can use sunlight to make oxygen and food. Seabirds and mammals that live in the sea breathe air at the surface of the water.

Most sea life is made up of tiny creatures and plants called plankton. They live in the sunlight near the top of the sea. Many sea animals, including the largest whales, eat plankton. There are fish in all the seas around the world. Most stay near the surface.

Molluscs, such as shellfish and octopus, sit at the bottom. Crustaceans, such as crabs and shrimp, also live on the bottom, eating bits of dead plants and animals that sink down.

Some of the creatures that live deep in the sea look very strange. This hatchetfish lights up.

DID YOU KNOW?

Coral reefs are found where there are shallow, warm waters. Many different creatures live on and around coral reefs. Corals reefs are made by millions of tiny coral polyps.

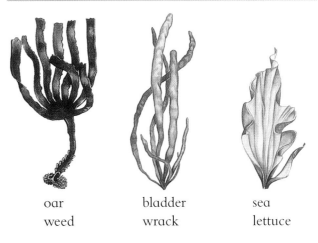

oar
weed

bladder
wrack

sea
lettuce

There are 7000 kinds of seaweed. They look very different in shape, size and colour. They can be used for food, fertiliser and to make medicines.

Sea lion

See also: Mammal, Sea life

A sea lion is a mammal which lives in the sea, but comes onto beaches to have its babies. Sea lions live in the Pacific and Atlantic Oceans. On land they can move faster than a person and they can swim up to 40 kph.

Sea lion families

A male sea lion is called a bull and a female sea lion is called a cow. A baby sea lion is called a pup. A bull marks out a territory and gets as many cows as possible to stay there. Each female has one pup at a time, and feeds it on milk for about six months. It is then old enough to hunt for its own food.

SEA LION FACTS

NUMBER OF KINDS	5
COLOUR	light brown
LENGTH	up to 2.2 m
WEIGHT	up to 275 kg
STATUS	common
LIFE SPAN	up to 15 years
ENEMIES	killer whales, people

Good eyes for seeing food

Ears to listen underwater for food

Long, smooth body to help push through the water

A South American sea lion

Back flippers to swim straight or turn quickly in the water

Strong front flippers for swimming fast

These Steller's sea lions are gathering on a beach to mate.

FOOD

A sea lion eats fish, squid and octopus. It can see very well, and chases its prey (animals it catches for food) through the water.

Sea urchin

See also: Sea life

A sea urchin is a ball-shaped animal, with a hard spiny skin. Sea urchins live in seas all over the world. They are one of the very oldest kinds of sea creature.

Sea urchin families

Sea urchins lay eggs. They send them floating off into the sea. The eggs hatch into tiny sea urchins. Adult sea urchins don't look after the eggs or the babies.

Sea urchins move around on hundreds of special tube feet. Each tube has suckers on it. These help the sea urchin grip onto underwater rocks.

SEA URCHIN FACTS

NUMBER OF KINDS	700
COLOUR	all
SIZE	5–30 cm across
STATUS	common
LIFE SPAN	about 10 years
ENEMIES	fish, people

Sharp spines to protect against enemies. Some sea urchins have poisonous spines

A sea urchin

Spines can grow again if they are snapped off

FOOD

A sea urchin scrapes up algae and small animals, such as coral, with the five moving pincers around its mouth.

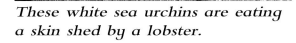

These white sea urchins are eating a skin shed by a lobster.

Seabird

See also: Bird, Gull

A seabird is any kind of bird that feeds in the sea. Gulls and terns are seabirds, and so are some ducks, geese and swans. Some seabirds, like the albatross, spend much of their life at sea. They only visit land to breed.

Seabird families

Different seabirds have different kinds of family life. All lay their eggs on land. Most have nests. Some nests are in trees or cliffs, others are on the beach or in the grass. Some seabirds nest in burrows in the ground. Both male and female seabirds feed their chicks.

SEABIRD FACTS

COLOUR......... mostly white, grey or black
LENGTH.......... 25 cm – 1.35 m
WEIGHT..........70 g – 12 kg
STATUS...........most are common
LIFE SPAN........5–30 years
ENEMIES..........Some land animals eat eggs and attack chicks.

FOOD

Most seabirds eat fish, squid or shellfish. Some seabirds can dive deep into the sea, but others pick up food close to the surface.

The puffin has a large and colourful bill. The bill can hold many small fish at one time.

The cormorant dives from the sky into the water to catch fish. It then has to dry its wings before it can fly properly again.

Seal

See also: Mammal, Sea lion

The seal is a mammal which lives in the sea. There are many kinds of seal all over the world. Many live in cold water and some in warm water. Fur seals have thick fur, but most seals have shiny waterproof short hair.

Seal families

A male seal is called a bull. A female seal is called a cow. A baby seal is called a pup. Bulls are usually much bigger than cows. Usually, the bulls swim to the land in the spring, before the cows, to choose a bit of land. Each bull tries to get cows to move onto his land.

A cow has only one pup each year. Pups are born with special furry coats to keep them warm. Cows feed their pups on milk until they can hunt for fish and squid.

SEAL FACTS

NUMBER OF KINDS	19
COLOUR	grey or brown
LENGTH	some kinds up to 5 m
WEIGHT	some kinds up to 2700 kg
STATUS	some are rare
LIFE SPAN	up to 38 years
ENEMIES	killer whales, people

Big eyes good for seeing in murky waters

Waterproof fur and thick blubber to keep warm in cold water

Flippers for swimming

A Southern fur seal

FOOD

Most seals eat fish, shellfish and squid. The leopard seal eats penguins. Seals can dive very deep under water to chase food.

These harp seal pups have white fur and cannot be seen in the snow.

Season

See also: Climate, Weather

Seasons are the different times of the year. Each season has its own kind of weather. They happen at about the same time every year.

The four seasons

Some places have four seasons: spring, summer, autumn and winter.

Spring: In spring the days are getting longer and plants are beginning to grow. Many farmers sow their seeds. Some animals mate in the spring. Others give birth.

Summer: It is warm and there is plenty of light in the summer. Days are long. Plants grow and make food for animals. Many animals raise their young.

Autumn: In the autumn the days are getting shorter. Crops are ripening and being harvested.

Winter: It is colder. Days are short and nights are long. Most plants stop growing. Some plants lose their leaves. There is less food for animals. Some animals hibernate and others migrate to warmer places.

DID YOU KNOW?

In the hot and wet parts of the world, near the equator, the days stay about the same length. Some places have no seasons at all. In tropical rainforests it is always hot and wet. Some deserts are always hot and dry.

In autumn, some types of trees have leaves which change into bright reds, oranges and yellows before they fall off.

Some places that don't have four seasons have dry and rainy seasons. This shows a storm during the rainy season in Malaysia.

Seed

See also: Crop, Plant

The seed is the part of a plant which may take root in the ground and grow into a new plant. Nuts and grains are seeds, and fruits have seeds inside them.

The life of a seed

A seed comes from a flower. As the flower's petals wilt and die, the seeds inside the flower swell and ripen. Birds, animals, water and the wind help to scatter different kinds of seeds. A new plant grows when a seed falls to the ground and starts to grow in the soil.

A seed contains a store of food. People and animals eat the seeds of many plants. Nuts are seeds protected by hard shells. Grain is the seed of wheat. It is ground into flour to make bread and pasta. Rice, beans, peas and sweetcorn are all seeds that can be cooked and eaten.

Stage 1 The root pushes its way out of the seed into the soil.

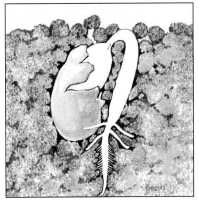

Stage 2 The root continues to grow. The stem begins to push its way out of the soil.

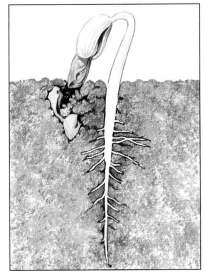

Stage 3 The stem has grown above the soil. Leaves start to grow out of the seed.

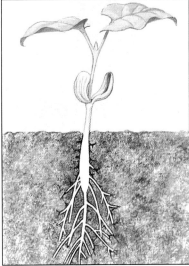

Stage 4 The root, stem and leaves have grown into a little plant.

These pictures show the four stages of the growth of a seed into a plant

Shark

See also: Fish

A shark is a fish. Different kinds of shark live in oceans and seas all over the world. Most sharks live in warm waters. The great white shark, the blue shark, the tiger shark and the leopard shark sometimes attack people.

Shark families

Little is known about shark families. The female shark gives birth to babies, which swim away on their own. Some kinds of shark have as many as 80 babies at a time!

The young sharks, called pups, stay close to the coasts and only go into deep water when they grow bigger.

SHARK FACTS

NUMBER OF KINDS	340
COLOUR	white, yellow, grey or blue
LENGTH	usually up to 6 m (whale shark 20 m long)
WEIGHT	usually up to 1200 kg (whale shark 7000 kg)
STATUS	great white is rare
LIFE SPAN	about 35 years
ENEMIES	Big sharks eat smaller sharks. Water pollution can hurt sharks.

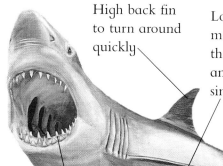

High back fin to turn around quickly

Long side fins move to keep the shark level and stop it sinking

Long tail swishes to build up speed

A great white shark

Sharp teeth used to hold and cut food

FOOD

A shark eats fish which it catches with its sharp teeth. Some sharks can smell blood in the water. Big sharks, like the tiger shark, will even eat turtles and seals. The world's biggest shark, the whale shark, eats only tiny creatures called krill and plankton.

The great white shark has two rows of sharp teeth.

Sheep

See also: Mammal

A sheep is a mammal. It has a long, warm, woolly coat and special feet so that it can live on mountains and hills. There are many different types of sheep. Farmers around the world keep sheep for their meat, milk and wool.

Sheep families

A male sheep is called a ram. A female sheep is called a ewe. A baby sheep is called a lamb. A ewe only has one or two lambs each year. Ewes and lambs, with one or two rams, live in a large group called a flock. In the wild, most rams will have a flock of their own. The female lambs stay in the flock after they have grown up. Most male lambs that are raised by farmers are sold for meat.

SHEEP FACTS

NUMBER OF KINDS	over 200
COLOUR	usually white or brown
HEIGHT	up to 1.4 m
LENGTH	up to 1.6 m
WEIGHT	up to 140 kg
STATUS	common
LIFE SPAN	up to 20 years
ENEMIES	wolves, eagles, crows.

Some rams have horns for fighting

Wool coat to keep warm

Soft, split hooves give good balance for walking on rocks and hard ground

A sheep

FOOD

A sheep eats grass and the leaves of small bushes. Some sheep have very tough mouths which help them to eat prickly leaves and thorns.

This flock of Merino sheep is grazing in New Zealand. There are 58 million sheep in New Zealand and only 3 million people.

Ship

See also: Barge, Port, Transport, Waterway

A ship is a vessel that travels over the sea. Some ships carry goods. These are called cargo ships. Giant ships called tankers carry oil. Many countries have ships that they use for protection or in wars.

The first ships

The first ships that we know of were built in Egypt at least 6000 years ago. The first sailing ships were built from wood or bundles of reeds. In the last 150 years ships have been built with engines. These are faster and more reliable than sailing ships. Today, big ships are built from steel.

People and ships

Ships are the cheapest and easiest way for large amounts of goods to be sent from one country to another. Until aeroplanes became widely used, almost all long-distance travelling was by ship.

DID YOU KNOW?

The first settlers who travelled from Europe to the United States and Australia made their journeys by ship. Today, most passenger ships are used for holidays, but ships called ferries travel shorter distances, carrying people and vehicles.

SHIP FIRSTS

FIRST SEA-GOING SHIP....	Ancient Egypt, 4000 BC
FIRST SHIP TO GO AROUND THE WORLD.......	*The Victoria* in 1522
FIRST STEAM-POWERED SHIP TO CROSS THE ATLANTIC OCEAN.........	*The Savannah* in 1819

This modern oil tanker has to be guided into port by smaller boats called tugs.

The first ships were small and made of wood. Ships and boats made the same way are still used in India for fishing.

Sikhism

Sikhism is a world religion. Its followers are called Sikhs. Sikh means 'learner'. The religion began in northwest India and part of Pakistan. It grew from the teachings of Guru Nanak, who lived nearly 600 years ago.

Beliefs and teachings

Guru Nanak was born in 1469 in the Punjab. When he grew up, he believed that God told him to show people how to follow a simple faith. Nine other gurus followed Guru Nanak. The tenth guru put all the teachings into a book called the Guru Granth Sahib.

Sikhs believe in one God, who is neither a man nor a woman, and is of no colour or rank. Sikhs think deeply about the meaning of God. They try to live their lives with honesty, hard work and caring.

Sikhism today

There are about 20 million Sikhs all over the world. Most live in India. Sikhs pray at home and in Sikh temples called *gurdwaras*. Food is also served in the *gurdwaras*. There are festivals called *gurpurbs*, that mark the anniversaries of the ten Sikh gurus.

Lots of food prepared in the kitchen of the Sikh temple is served at a Sikh wedding.

The Guru Granth Sahib is so important that it is kept on a throne and is looked after by a special person, called a granthi.

DID YOU KNOW?

Sikhs have five special symbols called 'The Five Ks'. They are worn by the Khalsa, who are groups of devout Sikhs.

Singapore

See also: Asia, Port

Singapore is a very small country in south-east Asia. Most of Singapore is on one big island. The weather is always hot and wet. There are some forests with monkeys and many types of butterfly.

Living and working

Most people work in banks and in other office jobs. Many women make parts for computers. Some people have jobs in the docks at the port.

People from China, Malaysia, India and other countries have come to live in Singapore. Each group has its own festivals. There are street parades with dragons and lanterns to celebrate the Chinese New Year.

There are many modern buildings in Singapore.

DID YOU KNOW?

The port of Singapore is the largest in the world.

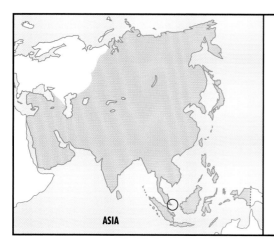

ASIA

FACT FILE

PEOPLE	Singaporean
POPULATION	2.8 million
MAIN LANGUAGES	English, Malay, Chinese, Tamil
CAPITAL CITY	Singapore City
MONEY	Singapore dollar
HIGHEST POINT	Bukit Tamah Hill – 176 m

Skeleton

See also: Human body, Vertebrate

A skeleton is the framework of bones that holds an animal up. It protects the important organs and helps the animal to move.

The human skeleton

The human body has over 200 bones joined to make a skeleton. Living cells make new bone as humans grow. In young babies many of the bones are not hard. They bend easily. In adults, the bones become more brittle. Old people's bones break quite easily.

Joints and moving

To move, the skeleton must have joints. Some joints between bones are like the hinges of a door. The bones can move but they stay fixed together. Ligaments are like strong strings that hold the bones together at the joints. Tendons are like ligaments, but they join the muscles to the bones. Bones are moved by muscles pulling on them.

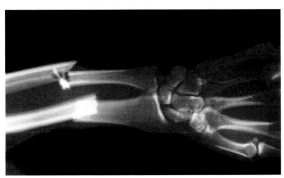

This X-ray shows an arm with two broken bones.

DID YOU KNOW?

Some animals have their skeleton on the outside. These are called exoskeletons. Shells are one sort of exoskeleton. An exoskeleton cannot grow. As the animal gets bigger it has to shed its skeleton and form another one.

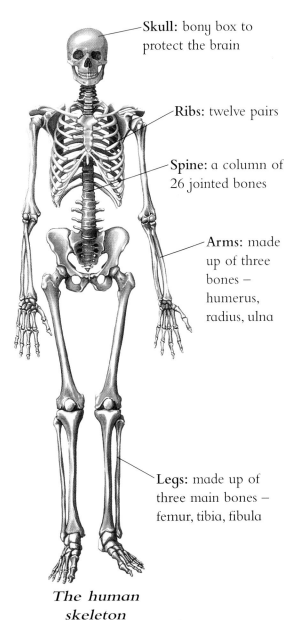

Skull: bony box to protect the brain

Ribs: twelve pairs

Spine: a column of 26 jointed bones

Arms: made up of three bones – humerus, radius, ulna

Legs: made up of three main bones – femur, tibia, fibula

The human skeleton

Skunk

See also: Mammal

The skunk is a mammal that hunts at night. It lives in North America. It is coloured black and white to warn off other animals. It sprays a horrible-smelling liquid on its enemies, or when it is frightened.

Skunk families

A skunk often lives in a pile of wood, in a home called a den. Sometimes it shares its den with a fox or racoon. The female skunk gives birth to between four and ten babies. These are called kits. She feeds them on milk. Even after they are old enough to hunt, kits stay with their mother until the next season. In the winter, several males and females share a den and can sleep or rest for several months.

SKUNK FACTS

NUMBER OF KINDS....13	
COLOUR....................	black and white
LENGTH....................	45 cm plus tail
WEIGHT....................	up to 3 kg
STATUS	common
LIFE SPAN.................	about 7 years
ENEMIES....................	bobcats, owls, people

Fur and fluffy tail to keep warm

Sharp claws for digging up food

Glands under the tail full of a nasty-smelling liquid to shoot at enemies

A skunk

Kits stay close to their den or their mother when they are young.

FOOD

A skunk digs in the soil to find insects such as grasshoppers and beetles. It also digs up worms, roots and fungi. A skunk will also claw fish out of the water.

Slovakia

See also: Europe, Czech Republic

Slovakia is a country in central Europe. There are many mountains with forests. Winters are cold. Summers are warm. It is hot on the flat land in the south.

Living and working

Most people in Slovakia live in the countryside. Farmers grow grapes, sugar beet, maize and wheat. There are factories where many people work making ceramics and machinery.

There are many traditional foods in Slovakia. The spice called paprika is cooked with beef and chicken. Pancakes are served, filled with chocolate sauce.

Slovakia is famous for making musical instruments. In the east of Slovakia there are folk music festivals. In Bratislava there are pop music festivals where local musicians perform.

St Martin's Cathedral in Bratislava is still one of the tallest buildings on the skyline.

DID YOU KNOW?

Until 1994, Slovakia and the Czech Republic formed the country of Czechoslovakia.

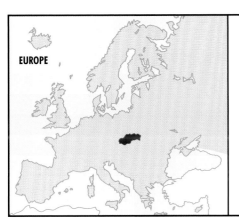

EUROPE

FACT FILE

PEOPLE................. Slovaks, Slovakians

POPULATION.......... 5.3 million

MAIN LANGUAGE... Slovak

CAPITAL CITY........ Bratislava

MONEY................. Koruna

HIGHEST POINT..... Gerlachovský Stít – 2654 m

LONGEST RIVER..... River Danube – 2850 km

Slovenia

See also: Yugoslavia

Slovenia is a country in south-east Europe. There are hills and mountains. There are many forests. Summers are warm. Winters are cold. The mountains have heavy snow.

Living and working

Half the people in Slovenia live in the cities and work in offices and factories. There are mines for coal, lead, zinc and mercury. In the countryside farmers grow cereals, potatoes and fruit. Some also raise sheep, goats and cattle.

In winter, the mountains are popular with tourists. Many people go there to ski.

A favourite meal in Slovenia is beans and pork, cooked with sauerkraut. Sauerkraut is pickled cabbage, chopped up. Pastries filled with cheese, apples, walnuts and poppy seeds, called *gibanica*, are also very popular.

At some weddings women wear highly decorated costumes with embroidered hats.

DID YOU KNOW?

Slovene, the language of Slovenia, has 40 different local forms. When the same language has different forms, they are called dialects.

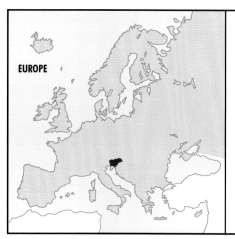

EUROPE

FACT FILE

PEOPLE	Slovenes, Slovenians
POPULATION	2 million
MAIN LANGUAGE	Slovene
CAPITAL CITY	Ljubljana
MONEY	Tolar
HIGHEST MOUNTAIN	Mount Triglav – 2863 m
LONGEST RIVER	River Sava – 940 km